T0104411

THE LITTLE GIRL WHO WANTED TO BECOME A DOCTOR...OF PHILOSOPHY!

Lisa Hairston

Order this book online at www.trafford.com
or email orders@trafford.com

Most Trafford titles are also available at major online book retailers.

Print information available on the last page.

ISBN: 978-1-4907-7392-6 (sc)
ISBN: 978-1-4907-7391-9 (e)

Trafford rev.   06/14/2016

Trafford PUBLISHING®   www.trafford.com
North America & international
toll-free: 1 888 232 4444 (USA & Canada)
fax: 812 355 4082

Word Of Warning!!!

The contents contained within this book – a combination of a children's book, short novel, and brief autobiography all rolled into one, of my real-life experiences with the topic of reading in question, as well as my desire to pursue a PH.D., and the dilemmas I faced in my attempts to reach my objective, contain GRE Vocabulary Words that might precipitate your need to consult a dictionary to look up each definition!!!

If you are, indeed, tempted to look up any or all of these words, my purpose in writing this book, *The Little Girl Who Wanted To Become A Doctor – Of Philosophy, is* a success!!!

I am an avid fan of Education, Higher Education, and life-long learning, and this book has been written to inspire individuals of all ages, particularly African-American parents, to spend more time reading in such a manner that reaching goals of the highest earthly degree would become inevitable, regardless of any or every obstacle standing in the way!!!

May each one of you continue to read out loud to one another!!!

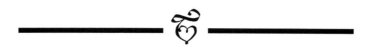

Dedication

I dedicate this book to the hundreds of thousands of African-Americans who stepped outside of the traditional, preconceived and perceived norm, and dared to think outside the box, to pursue their doctoral degrees, especially at a critical time in history when the majority of people of color I know refuse to read books, let alone read books out loud to their children.

None of the countless books that you have had to read, none of the infinite papers that you have had to write, none of the innumerable GRE Vocabulary Words that you have had to endlessly study, and none of the untold sacrifices that you have had to make in order to finally attain your remarkably, noteworthy objective have been in vain.

Reading is indeed a privilege, and you have mastered the art!!! I am writing this book so others like you will endeavor to think, act, read, write, and live like a Doctor of Philosophy – at an earlier age, so they, too, can give themselves every advantage life has to offer!!!

God Bless You!!!

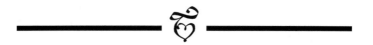

Foreword

What were you put on this earth to do? What talents and abilities do you possess? Which of these talents and abilities do you like best? And are you using any of these talents to the best of your ability, or have you settled for a life where you are forced to live out every day of your existence engaging in the kind of work that does not reflect what you do best?

These questions are the driving force behind this book, *The Little Girl Who Wanted To Become A Doctor…Of Philosophy!!! This book was designed to* illustrate how easy it is to be talked out of one's dream, especially if you are an African-American and you have no support system to keep you moving towards your goal!!!

This book was written for African-Americans as a baseline to determine where you are in your thinking. There can be no more excuses as to why we, as people of color, cannot succeed in the real world!!!

And there is no reason why any of us should not spend more time passing down to one another the power and gift of reading.

Reading is a privilege, and my goal as an African-American author is to author more books that feature African-American stories that would appeal to more and more African-Americans.

I have authored seven books to date, all of which convey inspirational messages to anyone of any race, age, or gender, however, I am hard pressed to put forth more of an effort in this, my eighth book, to discuss issues that are prevalent in the African-American community.

Personally, I have lost out on a lot of opportunities as an African-American female because of how I have been perceived by all races and people from all walks of life that I have encountered over the years.

I did not fit into anyone's school of thought. To them, I was either too ahead of my time, or I was not advanced enough. I was either too young or too old. I was either too bright or I was not bright enough.

And most importantly, all I ever heard was, "Wait until we get there!!!" As a result, I was left behind by individuals who never cared whether I "arrived" or not.

I am writing this book to catch up to where I would have been, should have been, and could have been, if I were permitted the occasion to write my own curriculum plan for my own life.

Moreover, there have been lots of speculation floating around as to whether or not standardized tests discriminate against minorities, particularly African-Americans.

In 1991, I enrolled in a private college to pursue a Bachelor's Degree in Special Education. I did exceptionally well in all my classes. I thought everything was set for me to receive my four-year degree.

Unfortunately, I failed the General Knowledge Section of the National Teacher's exam three times. I was devastated!!! I had spent the past three years looking forward to graduation. I shamefully and disgracefully left school without my degree in 1994.

I returned back to the same college in 2015, some 21 years later, endeavoring to receive a Bachelor's of Arts and Science Degree in Interdisciplinary Studies (B.A.S.I.S).

I had been conferring with my Online Graduate Program Advisors for months before my anticipated graduation, and all I needed was my four-year degree and I would have had an opportunity to pursue both my Master's and Doctorate Degrees.

Obstacles I cannot discuss due to confidentiality issues blocked my way in getting my degree this second time around. I was unable to remove my Incompletes in two of my three classes. I had run out of financial aid at the undergraduate level on top of everything else.

Had I gone to graduate school, I would have had enough financial aid at the graduate level to complete my goal of obtaining my Ph.D.! Once again, I was devastated!!!

Writing this book has been therapeutic for me. I can now let go of the past, and forge happily ahead as I carve out the life I knew I was destined to live – great!!! I have not given up my dream of becoming a Doctor of Philosophy, even though I am now 53 years of age.

All these years I believed that standardized tests discriminate against African-Americans. After all, I failed the NTE miserably on each of my three attempts.

What I did not know at the time is that in spite of my ability to read at a 6th Grade level by the time I was 5, no one read out loud to me on a daily basis.

No one at school, or anywhere else, bothered to tell me that I could have been spending the three years of my matriculation at college, and even years before then, reading more advanced reading material to improve my reading comprehension and expand my vocabulary.

No one bothered to tell me that most African-Americans fail standardized tests because no one read to them out loud on a daily basis.

Lastly, no one bothered to tell me that I would have passed the National Teacher's Exam the first time out had I been familiar with the format of any standardized tests questions, and had mastered the language.

All standardized tests have a language that can be mastered if people of color would take the time to expand their vocabulary base and spend adequate amounts of time practicing simulated study questions that might appear on the tests they are required to take.

I wrote the book, *The Little Girl Who Wanted To Become A Doctor...Of Philosophy* on purpose. I deliberately chose a 5-year old African-American girl to portray the main character of the story to highlight the steps she took to achieve her dream, despite the odds.

Hopefully, my testimony given here, coupled with the contents of this book, will provoke people of color to <u>rise up and read out loud to their loved ones, family, and friends like never before!!!</u>

And hopefully, someone in the education field will read my story and confer upon me several Honorary Doctorate Degrees to make up for all the years, and high income, that I lost out on, if not giving me a full scholarship to pursue additional degrees for free!!!

In conclusion, you are what you read, and you are what you hear. My greatest hope is that everyone reading this book will spend the rest of their lives reading out loud as if their very life depended on it!!!

Blessed is he that readeth, and they that heareth the words of this prophecy, and keep those things which are written therein, for the time is at hand. (Revelation 1:3)

Once upon a time, there was a little girl named Desiree Moore. She was so appropriately named because from a very early age – 5 to be exact – Desiree desired MORE out of life than adults thirteen times her age!!!

One day, Desiree made a profound and prolific statement that sent shock waves down everyone's spine. She vowed and averred emphatically, "When I grow up, I want to become a doctor!!!"

Everyone who was anyone only laughed in Desiree's face. "I simply cannot believe that you of all people want to become a doctor.

That is without a doubt the most absurd and ridiculous statement that anyone your age has ever made. Girl, what in the world were you thinking??? Get such a notion out of your head right now, young lady!!!"

Refusing to shed a tear, though she felt like crying right now, Desiree replied in the only manner she could: "I can, too, become a doctor!!! Just you watch and see!!! I will show you!!! I will show you all!!!"

Desiree became so angry she decided to storm out of the room in disgust, but not before hearing an entourage of millions of reasons why it was impossible for her to become a doctor.

Anyone who was anyone was determined to tell Desiree the truth. "First of all, Desiree, you are an African-American female. I do not want to be a bearer of bad news, but Black girls should not be thinking about becoming a doctor. Perhaps you should be a teacher, instead.

Secondly, look around you, Desiree!!! Clearly you were born on the wrong side of the tracks!!! Honey, this is the ghetto – the projects. Most people in these parts do not make it out of here alive. You would be wise to remember that!!!

Where do you think you are – Wall Street? And this is most definitely not Corporate America where Caucasian men wear a suit and tie, and you can see them walking to their fancy offices with a briefcase in their hands. Girl, please!!! You must think this is Easy Street!!!

Let us be real, Desiree. It is great that you have such a notable dream, but in case no one has told you, you are not smart enough to be a doctor!

You are not pretty enough! You are not bright enough! You are not good enough! And you are certainly not rich enough! Do you have any idea how expensive it is to be a doctor?

Again, Desiree, you are not the right age. It takes at least twelve years to become a doctor. How would you support yourself financially if you went to medical school?

You are not the right gender. In these parts, no patient wants to be seen by an African-American female doctor. It just would not be right.

And lastly, you are not from the right neighborhood or the right family. Most of the doctors you hear about went to one of those fancy colleges for rich kids. People like us cannot afford to go to any of those kinds of schools.

Do not think that I am being mean; I am just trying to spare you from future heartbreak. This is a White man's world, and in their world, you have to know your place. That is the way thing have always been and that is the way things will continue to be!!!

So get those silly thoughts of becoming a doctor out of your head. The only doctor you will ever see is the one you will visit if you ever get sick!!!

Besides, Desiree, even if you were to become a doctor, what kind of doctor would you become? You haven't given that much thought, have you? There are many kinds of doctors, and they specialize in different things."

Desiree had to admit that she, indeed, had no clue as to what kind of doctor she wanted to be. Would she become a neurosurgeon? Would she become a pediatrician? Would she become a cardiologist? Would she become a psychiatrist? Would she become a dentist? She did not have the answer to any of those questions. Perhaps she should just give the matter a little more thought.

For the moment, Desiree abandoned the idea of telling anyone else about wanting to become a doctor. At least until she had a clear picture of exactly what kind of doctor she would become! But, one thing was for certain!!! No one was going to talk her out of reaching her goal.

Desiree would never give up on her dream. She was absolutely sure that God had given her the desire to become a doctor in the first place, and it would be He who would give her direction in the path that she should take. Hadn't He always???

Mr. and Mrs. Moore had not raised a fool, and Desiree was by no means anybody's fool. If she were to be successful in becoming the doctor she wanted to be, Desiree would need a Plan of Action (P.O.A.), which she had.

Desiree's first order of business was to secure a mentor who would assist her in reaching the cardinal goal that she had set for herself. She needed an ally in her corner who would understand why becoming a doctor was of the utmost importance to her!

Alma Mater was the perfect candidate for the job, at least in Desiree's mind, meaning that Mrs. Alma Mater was the one person in the world who deemed her desire to become a Doctor of Philosophy worthy.

Mrs. Alma Mater held a Bachelor's degree in English, with a minor in Psychology. She also held a Master's degree in Library Science, and a Ph.D. in Education – all of which she earned from Harvard University.

On the same token, Mrs. Alma Mater was also working towards a second Doctorate in Educational Leadership at Harvard University. Mrs. Alma Mater's goal was to land her dream job – College President at a historically Black College.

Mrs. Alma Mater was so great at her profession, she could easily land a position at her Alma Mater, Harvard University. She had the brains and the talent, and all the students and faculty loved her.

Working at Harvard in any capacity was nothing to sneeze at!!! Many people she knew would love to be in such a position to even get their foot in the door.

Harvard only employed the best of the best, and she would have been hired on the spot at any time. All she had to do was speak the word and she "was in!!!"

Education mattered to Mrs. Alma Mater!!! She loved the teaching profession so much she would teach anyone of any age, race, gender, socio-economic status and religious affiliation.

However, working as a school librarian at the primary school where she was happily employed, Mrs. Alma Mater noticed one pertinent fact that even the school administrators and school board had overlooked – "or had they actually overlooked anything???" Mrs. Alma Mater wondered!!!

African-American students frequented her library on a regular basis throughout the week to borrow books they could read. The only problem was that none of the books housed in the school library featured books written by African-American authors, or any reading materials - hard covers or paper backs - published by African-American publishing companies!!!

Nor did any of the books on the shelves highlight the life, culture, ethnicity, or traditions of African-Americans. African-American children did not have anything to read that depicted what it was like to be African-American.

If one were to look at the media – particularly television, African-Americans were either portrayed as male criminals who were presently incarcerated in the prison system for drug trafficking, as butlers working within Caucasian homes, or slaves working on plantations in the deep south.

Very few television sitcoms displayed African-Americans living in such abodes as mansions, townhouses, condominiums, or any other equivalent, upscale housing facilities.

African-American women, wearing bandannas on their heads could be seen walking around with babies on their hips, cursing out "their baby's daddy."

Or in most cases, women of color were being portrayed as prostitutes or the girlfriends of "gang bangers" who were getting gunned down in drive-by shootings.

With respect to money, the word, "revenue," never escaped the lips of anyone living within the African-American community, better known as the "projects" or the "ghetto."

While both the middle class and the poor class citizens were focused on how to make it from paycheck to paycheck, the rich and famous were concerned about "generating revenue."

Virtually no one was writing about African-Americans outside of a few books here and there!!! The only exposure many African-American kids had to any person of color was Black History Month in February.

Why should any Black child have to wait until once a year to hear about the contributions African-Americans have made to society, and there have been many accomplishments achieved by African-Americans that still to this day continue to remain arcane to the majority of the world.

The world watched in astonishment at the election of 2008 as Barack Hussein Obama became the first African-American male to become the President of the United States of America. No one, Black or White, Republican, Democrat, or Independent, expected him to be re-elected to a second term in office.

When President Obama leaves office on January 20, 2017, he will leave behind an unprecedented legacy – one that should inspire anyone of any age, race, gender, etcetera, to want to aspire to higher ambitions.

Unfortunately, very few African-American students are being taught in the classrooms how to start their own legacy, or even their own business. Nor were they being taught to become great entrepreneurs!!!

Mrs. Alma Mater would do everything in her power to make sure that Desiree's legacy was not cut short before it even began. Unless she embarked upon her own dream of helping Desiree reach her goal, Desiree might just slip through the school system throughout her Prekindergarten to Post-Graduate School career, undetected.

Mrs. Alma Mater's heart was broken at the double standards, prejudices, and discriminating attitudes that Desiree was forced to endure. But, she had seen such "racism, sexism, ageism, and even Black-on-Black hatred before!!!

Every African-American could be heard expressing their outrage concerning police brutality occurring in the Black communities, especially that experienced by African-American males.

Pretty soon, if actions were not taken, African-American males could become extinct!!! But what about African-Americans who committed crimes against one another?

Many Black-on-Black crimes committed against one another – domestic violence, calling one another the "N" word, shootings, working against one another, sabotaging each other' success, not to mention envy and jealousy, were not being reported. Was this not genocide???

Was it not a crime for any African-American to wage war against their own child who wanted to become a Doctor of Philosophy???

How many times had Mrs. Alma Mater herself experienced such disdain from African-Americans who thought she had become "too uppity" because she sought a Ph.D.? She had persevered under such covert, verbal attacks, but could Desiree?

Mrs. Alma Mater would maintain her composure throughout the duration of serving as Desiree's mentor. It was deplorable to think that Desiree's parents, family, and acquaintances were not mentally, intellectually, or cognitively on board with Desiree's desire to become a Doctor of Philosophy.

Desiree, should she graduate from a four-year school, would be the first in her family to graduate from college. You would think that the Moore's would be thrilled that someone had "made it!!!"

Such was not the case. There were no "We are so proud of you's!!!" There were no exclamatory

"Congratulation's!!! There were no "Keep up the good work's" speeches!!!

Not one member of the Moore family could muster up enough strength, courage, or backbone to voice out loud one good reason why it was possible for Desiree to become a doctor.

As far as Mrs. Alma Mater was concerned, the Moore's giving Desiree one good reason why she could be a successful African-American female doctor was worth more in value than all the negative reasons they were sowing daily into Desiree's impressionable spirit as to why she could not become a Doctor of Philosophy!!!

Perhaps that is why Desiree had almost cried when Mrs. Alma Mater made it a point to read the following quote to Desiree out loud for the first time, but not the last: "Some people see things as they are and ask, 'Why?' I dream things that never were, and ask, 'Why not?'"

Desiree wanted MORE out of life, and she would never, like anyone in her family, settle for the status quo!!! Desiree wanted no part of mediocrity on any level.

And from Desiree's vantage point, her family and everyone in her daily, immediate space were expecting her to accept the same mediocrity they had given themselves over to.

Mrs. Alma Mater's reading the quote coined by George Bernard Shaw to Desiree out loud impacted the both of them instantaneously!!! Neither of them would be the same. The world, Desiree, and her family, not to mention her biggest critics, were about to witness a legacy unlike any other!!!

Most African-American parents were not adept in reading out loud to their children on a regular and consistent basis as were their Caucasian counterparts!!!

Is it any wonder that some African-American students did not fare well on standardized tests such as the SAT's, the GRE, the GMAT, and the NTE (National Teacher's Exam), now called Praxis.

Mrs. Alma Mater's Master's Degree in Library Science and Doctorate in Education were paying off with great dividends. She had access to the aforementioned assessments, and her academic training provided her with the necessary keys to unlocking the mysteries of such tests that alluded most African-American students on test day.

Much contention has centered around standardized tests and whether are not they, at any level, are discriminating to African-American students or to anyone that is not Caucasian.

Proponents of standardized tests maintain that the format of the questions more than adequately measure a student's ability to perform well both at school and on the job when they enter their chosen career.

Opponents of the test, on the other hand, maintain that many of the questions were designed to bar students of color from gaining access to equal opportunities such as being admitted into the college of their choice, landing that perfect job with excellent benefits, or empowering them to increase their earning potential.

That was the very reason Mrs. Alma Mater began reading out loud to Desiree every day without fail!!! Desiree would not have doors closed in her face because of an inability to master the language educational writers use when they devise and/or revise standardized test questions.

Thank God for big miracles!!! The Moore family reluctantly gave their permission for Mrs. Alma Mater to mentor their daughter, not that they thought that it would do Desiree any good.

But, perhaps they had realized one minute truth that Mrs. Alma Mater had passed on to them. Once upon a time, it was against the law for any slave to be caught reading.

If anyone from either the Caucasian or African-American race dared to teach slaves to read, the punishment could be severe. One was either flogged, or worse yet, lynched.

Now, it was very rare to persuade anyone of color to read – silently or out loud!!! Helping Desiree work towards her goal of becoming a doctor would at least give Mrs. Alma Mater the satisfaction of knowing that she had done all she could to ameliorate the present circumstances regarding many African-American's lack of love for reading.

May it be said here, however, that not all African-Americans view reading as a chore. How many hundreds of thousands of African-Americans did love to read?

Many an African-American PH.D. Candidate, as well as those pursuing a Doctoral Degree, had spent millions of hours, if not billions, learning GRE Vocabulary Words, reading literature at the highest of levels, writing countless papers, conducting endless research, and thinking critically about everything they put their hands to.

Many an African-American parent had read out loud to their children, but in such cases, this was an aberration, a deviation from the norm!!! More people of color needed to follow suit and commence the privilege of reading!!!

Desiree would not have to be coerced to read!!! She was born to read. Pretty soon, Desiree would realize that all Doctors of Philosophy were adept in reading everything they had privy to – especially more advanced reading material.

Curiosity had gotten the best of the Moore's, and they wanted to see how far all this reading out loud would take Desiree. Besides, the Moore's were right at the poverty line, and they did not really have any extra time on hand to read to Desiree themselves. "Wasn't it enough that they were working hard to keep a roof over Desiree's head???, asked the Moore's rhetorically.

If it were possible, Mrs. Alma Mater would love to meet the man, Jim Trelease, who authored the book, *The Read Aloud Handbook*, just so she could shake his hand. She wished she could literally put a copy of his book into the hands of every African-American living anywhere in the world.

The way Mrs. Alma Mater saw it, a certain percentage of African-Americans did not take the time to read books. They felt like they did not have the time. Nor did they think they had the necessary skill set to read out loud to their children.

According to Mr. Trelease, reading out loud to your child is much more effective than if your child reads silently on his or her own. When Mrs. Alma Mater surveyed students during the time she was conducting an extensive and intensive research to complete her dissertation, 99% of the students she interviewed confessed that they did not like to read, let alone read out loud to themselves!!!

Such a tragedy would not occur with Desiree!!! Mrs. Alma Mater would see to that!!! Immediately, Mrs. Alma Mater took Desiree to the local photography shop to have portraits of the both of them wearing a white cap and gown, simulating a mock graduate ceremony with Desiree receiving a mock Ph.D.!

The real mentorship program had gotten underway!!! Desiree Moore was officially her primary protégé, her only protégé, at least until after Desiree had graduated at the top of her Doctoral class.

Desiree had not only verbalized her intent to become a Doctor of Philosophy, she had sat down to physically write her Mission Statement:

"I Desiree Moore, hereby decree and declare, on this day, May 9, 2016, that I intend to become a Doctor of Philosophy, and I am willing to put in as much time as needed, now, to prepare for such a glorious event.

I realize that I am only five years old, but, I will not allow my young age, to deter me from my goal. Nor will I permit anyone of any age, present or future, to talk me out of my desire to become a Doctor of Philosophy.

As of today, I will conduct myself as if I am already a Doctor of Philosophy. I am not going to become a Doctor of Philosophy; I already am a Doctor of Philosophy, now. I will walk like a Doctor, I will talk like a Doctor, I will act like a Doctor. I will live like a Doctor, I will think like a Doctor, and I will read and write like a Doctor – because I am a Doctor – of Philosophy!!!"

From that moment on, Desiree was never really the same. Her whole personality and demeanor had changed. Her confidence level was escalating beyond anyone's expectations.

Day after day, and night after night, Desiree literally gave herself over to learning the following 500 GRE Vocabulary Words and committing them to memory until they oozed out of every pore of her body, which is what she wanted:

Abate	Allude
Aberration	Amalgamate
Abeyance	Ameliorate
Abjure	Amenable
Abrogate	Anachronistic
Abstemious	Analogous
Abstruse	Ancillary
Accolade	Anomaly
Accretion	Antagonism
Acerbic	Antipathy
Acquiesce	Apathy
Acumen	Apocryphal
Admonish	Apostate
Adroit	Apposite
Adulation	Apprise
Adulterate	Approbation
Aesthetic	Appropriate
Aggregate	Arcane
Alacrity	Archaic
Alleviate	Arduous

Articulate

Ascetic

Asperity

Aspersion

Assiduous

Assuage

Astringent

Asymmetrical

Atrophy

Attenuate

Attrition

Audacious

Auspicious

Austere

Autocratic

Autonomy

Avarice

Aver

Avid

Axiomatic

Baleful

Balk

Banality

Bane

Belabor

Belie

Bellicose

Beneficent

Betoken

Blatant

Blithe

Bode

Bolster

Bombastic

Bowdlerize

Broach

Brook

Burgeon

Burnish

Buttress

Byzantine

Cabal

Cacophonous

Cajole

Calumny

Candor

Canon

Cant

Capricious

Cardinal

Carping

Castigation

Catalyst

Categorical

Cathartic

Caustic

Cavalier

Cavil

Charisma

Charlatan

Chary

Chasten

Chauvinist

Chicanery

Chimerical

Circumlocution

Circumscribe

Clemency

Coalesce

Coda

Cogent

Cognizance

Commensurate

Commodious

Compendium

Complaisant

Complement

Compliant (1)

Compliant (2)

Comprise

Concerted

Concurrent

Condone

Confound

Connoisseur

Consistency

Contention

Contentious

Contingent (1)

Contingent (2)

Contrite

Convention

Converge

Convoluted

Correlation

Countenance

Craven

Credulity

Curmudgeon

Cursory

Daunt

Decorum

Definitive

Deleterious

Denigrate

Derisive

Derivative

Desiccate

Desultory

Diatribe

Dichotomy

Didactic

Diffidence

Dilatory

Disabuse

Disinterested

Disparate

Dissemble

Dissonance

Distend

Divine

Dogmatic

Dormant

Ebullient

Eclectic

Edify

Efficacy

Effrontery

Elicit

Embellish

Empirical

Emulate

Encomium

Endemic

Enervate

Engender

Enumerate

Ephemeral

Epitome

Equanimity

Equivocal

Erudition

Esoteric

Eulogize

Euphemism

Exacerbate

Exact

Exculpate

Exegesis

Exemplar

Exigency

Exonerate

Extrapolation

Facetious

Fallacious

Fatuous

Fawning

Felicitous

Fervor

Flag

Fledgling

Florid

Flout

Foment

Forbearance

Forestall

Fortuitous

Founder

Fractious

Frenetic

Furtive

Gainsay

Garner

Garrulous

Genre

Germane

Grandiloquent

Gratuitous

Gregarious

Guile

Hackneyed

Harangue

Harbinger

Hedonist

Hegemony

Hermetic (1)

Hermetic (2)

Heterodox

Heterogeneous

Hierarchy

Homogeneity

Hubris

Hyperbole
Iconoclastic
Idiosyncrasy
Idolatrous
Idyllic
Ignominious
Illusory
Immutable
Impassive
Impecunious
Imperiousness
Impermeable
Imperturbable
Impervious
Impetuous
Impiety
Implacable
Importune
Impregnable
Impugn
Impunity
Inchoate
Incipient
Indefatigable
Indeterminate
Indifferent
Indigent
Inert
Inexorable
Ingenuous
Inherent
Innate

Innocuousness
Insensible
Insipid
Insularity
Intractable
Intransigence
Intrepid
Inundate
Inure
Invective
Inveigle
Irascible
Irresolute
Itinerant
Jettison
Jingoist
Jocular
Juxtaposition
Kindle
Kinetic
Lachrymose
Laconic
Lassitude
Latent
Laud
Lethargic
Levity
Libertine
Limn
Listless
Loquacious
Lumber

Luminous

Machination

Magnanimity

Malevolent

Malinger

Malleable

Maverick

Mendacious

Mercenary

Mercurial

Metamorphosis

Meticulous

Minatory

Misanthrope

Mitigate

Mollify

Morose

Mundane

Munificent

Myopic

Myriad

Nascent

Nebulous

Nefarious

Neophyte

Nominal

Nonplus

Nuance

Obduracy

Obsequious

Obstinate

Obstreperous

Obviate

Occlude

Officious

Onerous

Opaque

Opportune

Opportunist

Opprobrium

Oscillate

Obstensible

Ostentation

Overt

Overwrought

Palliate

Palpable

Panegyric

Paradox

Paragon

Pariah

Parody

Parsimony

Partisan

Paucity

Peccadillo

Pecuniary

Pedagogy

Pedantic

Pejorative

Penchant

Penury

Perennial

Perfidious

Perfunctory

Peripatetic

Permeable

Peruse

Pervasive

Phenomena

Phlegmatic

Pithy

Placate

Plasticity

Platitude

Plethora

Plummet

Polemical

Politic

Porous

Pragmatic

Precarious

Precipitate

Preclude

Precursor

Predilection

Presumptious

Prevaricate

Pristine

Probity

Problematic

Proclivity

Prodigality

Profligacy

Proliferation

Propensity

Propitiate

Propriety

Prosaic

Proscribe

Pundit

Pungent

Pusillanimous

Quagmire

Qualified

Quell

Querulous

Quiescent

Quixotic

Quotidian

Rancor

Rarefied (1)

Rarefied (2)

Recalcitrant

Recant

Reclusive

Recondite

Redoubtable

Redress

Refractory

Refute

Rejoinder

Relegate

Reprehensible

Reprobate

Repudiate

Rescind

Restive

Reticent

Rhetorical

Rue

Sagacious

Salient

Salubrious

Salutary

Sanction

Sanguine

Sardonic

Satiate

Secrete

Sedulous

Sentient

Shard

Sinecure

Slake

Solecism

Solicitous

Sophistry

Soporific

Specious

Sporadic

Spurious

Static

Stentorian

Stigma

Stint

Stipulate

Stolid

Substantiate

Succinct

Supplant

Surfeit

Sybarite

Sycophant

Tacit

Taciturn

Tangential

Tantamount

Tenacity

Tenuous

Terse

Tirade

Torpor

Tortuous

Tout

Tractable

Transgression

Transient

Trenchant

Truculence

Turgid (1)

Turgid (2)

Tyro

Unconscionable

Unequivocal

Untenable

Vacillate

Variegated

Venerate

Veracious

Verbose

Verisimilitude

Vestigial
Viable
Virtuosity
Virulent
Viscous
Vituperative
Volatile

Voluble
Voracious
Welter
Whimsical
Zealot
Zenith

These terms were not inclusive of all the vocabulary words that Desiree wanted to learn, but they merely served as a precursor of all the thousands, if not millions, that were to come. These were only a repertoire of vocabulary words that would help Desiree get started on her quest of becoming a Doctor of Philosophy.

The Moore's were becoming worried and apprehensive about Desiree and her "so called GRE Words." Maybe learning them was a waste of time, and not age-appropriate for a 5-year old!!!

Perhaps the school board was right!!! Perhaps Desiree should be playing with Barbie Dolls instead!!!

How were they to know that these 501+ words would demonstrate that their Desiree could master the language a graduate student would need to know prior to being admitted into a graduate program?

If Desiree could not master the English language prior to taking the Graduate Record Examination, she would not do well on the exam. Then, her chances of becoming a Doctor of Philosophy would be thwarted.

Desire did not desire to balk at becoming a Doctor of Philosophy. She would not begin the tedious process of studying and absorbing GRE Vocabulary Words and their meanings, only to come to a complete halt – no matter what her age!!! She would carry every word she learned with her for the rest of her long life, and she expected to reach the young age of 150!!!

Mrs. Alma Mater knew what it took to become a Doctor of Philosophy. And she certainly knew what kind of toll so much studying could have on anyone at such an intense level, especially for a five-year-old.

But, Desiree was resilient. She absorbed new information like a sponge!!! She was to the education world what Mozart was to the music industry – a head of his time. And people were still, in essence, playing musical chairs trying to keep up with his legacy!!!

Was some Kindergarteners not learning Spanish as a second language at such a young age, proving that they could retain such knowledge at a higher rate than adult students learning a second language?

Unlike Mozart, Desiree would not be considered as a social misfit, meaning that Mozart was a musical genius, but lacked in social skills.

Academically, many Ph.D. Candidates dropped out of their Graduate Programs of Study before completing all the necessary requirements to receive their Ph.D. They could not hold up under all that pressure. The demand was much too great, and many Ph.D. Candidates had felt as if they had gotten in over their heads.

Such individuals, in more cases than none, did not have the emotional support needed to see the Doctoral Degree through to the end. The same was true of Desiree, with one significant exception. She had found a support system, exclusively in Mrs. Alma Mater.

The 501 words that Desiree was learning was not a one-time deal. Mrs. Alma Mater read the vocabulary words out loud to Desiree every day, even on the holidays. Satan and God never took one day of vacation, and neither would Desiree's education.

In the hours just before Desiree's bedtime, Desiree would retire to her room to listen to the vocabulary words on the CD's that Mrs. Alma Mater had recorded. She often fell asleep listening to them.

Desiree listened to these CD's each night, in addition to the myriad of Bedtime stories that Mrs. Alma Mater had also pre-recorded. These were not the "Cinderella" or "Hansel and Gretel" kind of stories. These were the kind of stories that would spark the interest of any African-American child, and motivate them to aspire to higher goals and objectives.

Mrs. Alma Mater was a *Best-Selling, Published Author,* and she spent a lot of time reading the inspirational books and novels that she had written out loud to Desiree. She was also hoping that one of her books, would lead to an exclusive, lucrative movie deal.

At least 99% of her books depicted African-Americans achieving success at the highest end of the spectrum!!!

Moreover, Mrs. Alma Mater was not clueless as to the millions of ways a child prodigy such as Desiree could be hindered at reaching her goal of becoming a Doctor of Philosophy.

Some African-Americans had once been compared to crabs in a bucket. As soon as one of the crabs managed to make it to the top of the barrel, one or more of the other crabs would pull it back down to the bottom.

"Did these crabs not know that such actions were meaningless and a waste of time?"

As long as each crab spent so much time pulling one another down, none of them would ever get out of the barrel.

The same principle holds true for African-Americans. As long as African-Americans strive to pull one another down, no one in the entire race is really getting anywhere!!!

Desiree's parents had unintentionally caused more harm than good to Desiree by calling her every name in the book but a child of God!!! Obviously, they had not read Lisa Lee Hairston's book, *What You Say To Your Child Really Does Matter!!!*

Desiree's parents should have said, "You would be the very first person in our family to become a Doctor of Philosophy. You are the brightest student in your class. You are anachronistic, which in this case means that Desire was ahead of her time.

If anyone can become a Doctor, it is you Desiree, and though it may take at least twelve years for you to literally become a Doctor of Philosophy, you could always take out college loans to help finance your way through school.

Better yet, as intelligent as you are, you could make so much money because of your talents and abilities that you could earn enough money to pay for the total cost of your education in cash, and not have to borrow one red cent. We will do everything in our power to help you!!!

You could even get a full-scholarship to Harvard University!!!

Yes, we live here in the projects, but your brains alone could get you out of here. We are so excited about all the possibilities that are open to you as an African-American female.

Who knows!!! You might just become the first African-American Female President of the United States of America. We could all end up living in the Whitehouse at 1600 Pennsylvania Avenue in Washington, D.C. Hallelujah!!!"

All of Desiree's hard work was paying off. She was being noticed by her teachers and school administrators, all of whom encouraged her to enter the school's Spelling Bee.

Year after year, Desiree won the State Championship, always defeating the best and brightest, not to mention the most formidable international contestants. Such an impressive academic career began in Kindergarten.

"Desiree, to whom or what do you attribute to your obvious success? You are only 5 years old, and according to the school district, your Intelligence Quotient is so high, you will skip primary school next year to attend Harvard University to pursue a Ph.D. In Education. How does that make you feel???," asked the news reporter!!!

"Everyone I speak to thinks that I am some sort of freak of nature. They think I am much too young to be attending Harvard University.

But, I once read of a man who was speaking fluently at six months of age, and he later dropped out of school because he knew more than his college professors. If I am not mistaken, that man had an IQ of 210. My IQ is exponentially higher!!!

I owe my success first of all to God, my Creator. It was he who instilled in me an innate love for learning. Secondly, I contribute my success to my mom and dad who allowed Mrs. Alma Mater to mentor me (Desiree was much to gracious to speak ill of her biggest critics)!!!

Have you ever read any of Lisa Lee Hairston's seven books? I know Lisa Lee Hairston personally, and she had the goal of receiving several Doctorate degrees, but because she was so brainy, she was told that she was too smart for her own good!!!

By the time she was in the 1st Grade, she was already reading beyond a 6th Grade Level, but no one helped her, so she was forced to stifle her inner academic giftings.

Lisa received her two-year college degree in 1991, and thereafter pursued a Bachelor's Degree in Special Education. Three years into the program, she failed the National Teacher's Exam three times, and she left college in 1994 without her four-year degree.

In 2015, she re-entered her prospective Alma Mater, where she changed her major to pursue her Bachelor's Degree in Interdisciplinary Studies (Bachelor of Arts and Sciences in Interdisciplinary Studies).

She was three classes away from completing her degree, and she was already making plans to pursue a Master's and Doctorate Online.

She was put in a position where she could not finish her three classes or remove the two incompletes from her transcript by the time allotted. Whatever happened to her?

Lisa ended up barely landing a housekeeping position in a nursing home facility, earning $7.50 an hour. It was impossible for her to finish her degree because of extenuating circumstances beyond her control. No one seemed to care about the plight of a non-traditional student that was now 53 years of age.

You would have thought that under such extenuating circumstances as I previously mentioned that someone at school would have given Lisa a big break and just given her the 4-year degree. But, no one did, at least not to date!!!

Though Lisa could read beyond a 6th Grade Level by the time she was in 1st Grade, no one read out loud to her on a daily basis. I believe that is why she did not do well on the NTE's or any other Standardized tests.

When Lisa's much younger peers at college heard Lisa's story as to why she could not pass the National Teacher's Exam, they felt so sorry for her, they endeavored to spend more time both reading for pleasure, and reading out loud to their own children when they became parents!!!

Today, Lisa is studying the GRE Vocabulary Flash Cards that Mrs. Alma Mater gave to me. Someday, she will get her Ph.D., but in the meantime, I am using her story to inspire me to help others just like Lisa.

This Summer, I will be Starting my new Business Venture: I will be opening up "The Reading Agency." For a nominal fee, I will be reading out loud to children so they can develop powerful reading comprehension skills.

Lisa presented a topic at school concerning how Freshmen at historically black colleges should be preparing to pursue a doctorate during their first week on campus, and it was met with nothing short of disdain. But, one valuable lesson was learned.

Nothing Lisa did to further her research on doctorate programs worked. She was stone walled, especially by individuals holding a Master's or Doctorate Degrees. She was told she was too smart.

Lisa wanted to write a dissertation just for the fun of it, but she was told she would have to wait until she was a Doctoral Candidate.

She went to the public library to borrow copies of published dissertations to read in her leisure, in the privacy of her own home, but she was told she would have to read any published dissertations at the University library that housed dissertations.

Lisa's intent was to browse over every dissertation with a fine-tooth comb, so to speak, so that she could master the mechanics of writing an "A" Dissertation.

That is why Mrs. Alma Mater read the GRE Vocabulary Words to me out loud!!! That is why she read her own published dissertation out loud to me!!! That is why Mrs. Alma Mater took me on field trips to the University library daily for the past year – to sit with me while I read dissertation after dissertation.

As far as Desiree was concerned, published dissertations should be made readily available to the public, especially to libraries.

Mrs. Alma Mater once told me that if I studied anything daily and consistently for one year, I would become an expert in just a year. That is why she made it her top priority to make sure I got to the library every day that they were open.

On many occasions, the college librarian let Mrs. Alma Mater and me borrow countless dissertations to read for months on end before having to return them back to the library.

They saw my determination to become a Doctor of Philosophy, and they joined the cause of helping me to do everything in my power to achieve my goal.

They did not want to be viewed as putting up any seen and unseen barriers to block my success. They went out on a limb and granted me access to every tidbit of information they had on hand.

Because I had access to dissertations and other high-level reading material, I learned how to think critically, which expanded my already impressive reading comprehension.

I learned how to think, act, read, write and live like a Doctor of Philosophy - all while I was 5. And most importantly, I was able to conduct advanced, original research that lead to a dissertation proposal that no one else had ever thought of – the purpose of a Doctor of Philosophy writing a dissertation in the first place.

In conclusion, I am a better person because I learned how to think like a Doctor of Philosophy <u>BEFORE</u> I became a Ph.D. Candidate. I plan to impart that same acumen on to the next generation. I never thought I could change the face of education!

Oh, and one last thought on that subject. I have noticed that individuals holding a Doctorate Degree of any sort have a tendency to safe guard the knowledge they have obtained, refusing to pass on what they have learned to others.

It is as if they have adopted the mentality that, I've gotten mine, and you get yours!!! But, I am not going to do anything to help you get yours. If anything, I will stand in your way so that you cannot get your Doctorate Degree."

Did these graduates have such difficulty getting their degree that they would impede the progress of any prospective Ph.D. Candidate that might do so more easily.

If so, are these individuals who have "arrived" better off than those African-Americans who fail to read at all? Would these graduates not want to make the road easier for successive generations to come? Perhaps I need to conduct more research to uncover the answer to such thought-provoking questions!!!

Tears flowed down Desiree's eyes!!! This was only the second time in her six-year lifespan that she had cried. The only other time she had lost her composure was the day her parents had so callously, cold-heartedly, and unsympathetically debriefed her on becoming a Doctor of Philosophy because they thought they were doing her a great service.

Desiree Moore had proved her parents, closest relatives, and worst critics wrong!!! Today, both she and Mrs. Alma Mater, whom she now respectfully and reverentially referred to as Dr. Alma Mater, were seated in the auditorium of the larger than life historically Black College Campus.

The exceptional African-American College President was about to confer upon both she and Dr. Alma Mater their second Honorary Doctorate – a feat no other person of any race had ever accomplished in human history.

Desiree stole a glance at Dr. Alma Mater. She, too, grasped the significance of such an earth-shattering, pivotal, and historical moment.

In the same way that Chuck Yeager had broken the sound barrier on October 14, 1947, Desiree and her beloved mentor had broken educational barriers.

Outside of herself and Dr. Alma Mater, who would have ever guessed that a young, African-American girl who had just turned 5 when she made the quality decision to become a Doctor of Philosophy, would receive her Ph.D. in Education from Harvard University at the mere age of 6?

And who would have ever guessed that Desiree Moore would also receive two Honorary Doctorate Degrees as well?

Desiree's mind reflected on the following information entitled, *Doctorate of Philosophy In Education* which she had, with Dr. Alma's assistance, happily downloaded from the Harvard University Website, https://www.gse.harvard.edu/doctorate on the same unprecedented day that she had categorically decided to become a Doctor of Philosophy:

"The complex challenges facing 21st-century education require researchers who can collect and analyze information from multiple academic disciplines — economics, biology, psychology, the arts, history, and more — and translate those findings into transformative ideas for education policy reform and practice.

The Ph.D. in Education is an interdisciplinary doctoral program offered jointly by the Harvard Graduate School of Education and the Harvard Graduate School of Arts and Sciences.

As a Ph.D. candidate, you will enjoy unrestricted access to collaborate with scholars across all Harvard graduate schools on original interdisciplinary research. In the process, you will help forge new fields of inquiry that will impact the way we teach and learn.

In the fall of 2014, HGSE transitioned from conferring a Doctor of Education (Ed.D.) to conferring a Doctor of Philosophy (Ph.D.) in Education. The Ph.D. in Education, a joint degree offered in collaboration with Harvard's Graduate School of Arts and Sciences, replaced the Ed.D. to better signal the research emphasis that has characterized the program since its inception in 1921, and to strengthen ties with academic departments across Harvard University.

Graduates of the Ed.D. and Ph.D. in Education programs receive equally rigorous scholarly training. The requirements for both degrees include coursework that develops both knowledge that reflects the interdisciplinary nature of education and expertise in the range of quantitative and qualitative methods needed to conduct high-quality research.

Guided by the goal of having a transformative impact on education research, policy, and practice, our graduates focus their independent research in various domains, including human development, learning and teaching, policy analysis and evaluation, institutions and society, and instructional practice.

Graduates of both programs have and will assume roles as university faculty, researchers, senior-level education leaders, and policymakers.

As a Ph.D. candidate, you will choose from three concentrations that address some of the most significant questions in education: How do we learn? What is the role of education and schools in society? How do we develop the most effective education policies and programs? Once you choose a concentration, you will embark on an interdisciplinary research project that draws on faculty expertise and resources from across all Harvard graduate schools.

Harvard is an intellectual powerhouse in fields as varied as education, business, law, public policy, psychology, medicine, neuroscience, religious studies, and more. The Ph.D. in Education formalizes the scholarly relationships across schools and gives you full access to some of the most creative and influential thinkers in the world.

The questions you will explore in the Ph.D. Program have critical relevance in the field of education. Your research will benefit greatly from the extraordinary relationships HGSE has forged with leading policymakers and educators on the front lines of policy and practice, from an individual classroom teacher in Boston to the minister of education of a large African nation.

The Ph.D. in Education requires five years of full-time study to complete. You will choose your individual coursework and design your original research in close consultation with your HGSE faculty adviser and dissertation committee. The Ph.D. curriculum includes the following requirements and milestones:

During the first two years of the Ph.D., you will take a minimum of 16 courses, including:

- The Ph.D. Proseminar
- One (1) concentration core course
- At least four (4) research methods courses: two courses in quantitative methods, one course in foundational qualitative methods, and an additional course of your choosing in qualitative methods
- Reading time (equivalent to one course) in preparation for the written portion of the Comprehensive Exam

- Up to nine (9) additional elective courses, selected from HGSE and all Harvard graduate schools

The doctoral colloquia runs the full length of the program. Students in years one and two are required to attend. The colloquia meets weekly and features presentations of work-in-progress and completed work by Harvard faculty, faculty and researchers from outside Harvard, and Harvard doctoral students. Ph.D. students present twice in the colloquia over the course of their career.

The research apprenticeship also runs the full length of the Ph.D. Program. It is designed to provide ongoing training and mentoring to develop students' research skills.

The comprehensive exams are comprised of the Written Exam, which tests students on both general and concentration-specific knowledge, and the Oral Exam, designed to test students' command of their chosen field of study and their ability to design, develop, and implement an original research project.

Your final two years in the Ph.D. Program will focus on writing your dissertation based on original research. The dissertation process consists of three parts: the dissertation proposal, the writing of the dissertation, and an oral defense before the members of your dissertation committee.

Ph.D. students affiliate with one of three concentrations, each representing a fundamental field of inquiry that addresses critical questions in education reform.

Culture, Institutions, and Society (CIS)

In CIS, you will examine the broader cultural, institutional, organizational, and social contexts relevant to education across the lifespan. What is the value and purpose of education? How do cultural, institutional, and social factors shape educational processes and outcomes? How effective are social movements and community action in education reform? How do we measure stratification and institutional inequality? In CIS, your work will be informed by theories and methods from sociology, history, political science, organizational behavior and management, philosophy, and anthropology. You can examine contexts as diverse as classrooms, families, neighborhoods, schools, colleges and universities, religious institutions, nonprofits, government agencies, and more.

Education Policy and Program Evaluation (EPPE)

In EPPE, you will research the design, implementation, and evaluation of education policy affecting early childhood, K-12, and postsecondary education in the U.S. and internationally. You will evaluate and assess individual programs and policies

related to critical issues like access to education,
teacher effectiveness, school finance, testing and
accountability systems, school choice, financial aid,
college enrollment and persistence, and more. Your
work will be informed by theories and methods
from economics, political science, public policy, and
sociology, history, philosophy, and statistics. This
concentration shares some themes with CIS, but
your work with EPPE will focus on public policy
and large-scale reforms.

Human Development, Learning and Teaching (HDLT)

In HDLT, you will work to advance the role of
scientific research in education policy, reform, and
practice. New discoveries in the science of learning
and development — the integration of biological,
cognitive, and social processes; the relationships
between technology and learning; or the factors that
influence individual variations in learning — are
transforming the practice of teaching and learning
in both formal and informal settings. Whether
studying behavioral, cognitive, or social-emotional
development in children or the design of learning
technologies to maximize understanding, you will
gain a strong background in human development,
the science of learning, and sociocultural factors
that explain variation in learning and developmental
pathways. Your research will be informed by
theories and methods from psychology, cognitive
science, sociology and linguistics, philosophy,

the biological sciences and mathematics, and organizational behavior."

These enlightening and didactic words were like music to her ears. What an epiphany!!! What a well-orchestrated symphony of verbiage. These glorious words were the epitome of her supra-brilliant mind!!!

Desiree had tried diligently and assiduously to refrain herself from downloading the encyclopedia of information from Harvard's Website, but she could not. She wanted to commit every single word to memory!!!

Subsequently, this was not the coda, the conclusion, the epilogue, or the grand finale of Desiree's great academic career!!! It was only the genesis of the next centillion chapters in her life. Hallelujah!!!

Desiree's desire to become a Doctor of Philosophy was only a tip of the iceberg and a hint of greater things ahead!!!

For Desiree, there would always be More – MUCH, MUCH MORE!!! While the rest of the world were attempting to get to where she had already been academically at only 5 – backtracking themselves to commit thousands of GRE Vocabulary Words to memory, and struggling to revamp the whole approach to a compulsory education by conclusively deciding what was considered academically age-appropriate, etcetera, Desiree would retire, if you will.

Prior to receiving her second Honorary Doctorate, Desiree had visited every single Historically Black College in the world – foreign and domestic.

She had conducted billions of interviews in billions of homes, all in the effort of getting individuals of all ages to vow to spend more hours reading out loud to themselves and to loved ones.

Most people hated the sound of their own voice, at first. They were not used to reading any other way than silently, if they read anything at all.

But, be that as it may, aggregate numbers of African-Americans, in particular, were seeing the value of reading out loud. 100% of the people she spoke to was so adamant about reading at a higher level, each person signed a contract to read for a billion hours, faithfully vowing to record each hour they read for future reference.

Again, who would have ever thought that a 5-year old African-American girl would be so academically bright that she would complete a Doctorate of Philosophy Degree by the age of 6?

Who could have ever guessed that Desiree was so gifted intellectually that educational administrators and the school board, as well as the State Department of Education, would have no choice but to pass her straight to the Ph.D. Program?

And who would have ever imagined that Desiree, once admitted to the Graduate Program would only need to submit one "A" Dissertation to the Graduate School Committee to satisfy graduation requirements?

Desiree had successfully written three dissertations – from start to finish!! While others had been playing with Barbie dolls and easy bake ovens, her precious GRE Vocabulary Words had been her closest companions.

Now, she could afford to take a break and catch up on her socialization, if that were possible. She had, after all, just flown back from the United Nations, where she had just been asked to serve as the International Minister of International Education.

Educators and Educational Administrators from every corner of the globe wanted in on Desiree's success.

No one would wonder anymore if it were appropriate for a girl Desiree's age to forego play and social interaction to carve out an academic career it would take students in their 20's, 30's, 40's, 50's and even 60's and beyond five lifetimes to complete. No one was as well socialized as Desiree Moore!!!

Desiree did not do "compulsory" or "sequential." Had she "waited until she got there [the doctoral program] to prepare herself to prepare for a Ph.D., she would not have gotten there!!!

And perhaps others who would not have gotten a Doctoral Degree anyway would have surpassed her dedication, if they made it to the program at all.

But, in any respect, Desiree had taken charge of her own life. She had not allowed the "have not's" to dictate to her what she could and could not do!!!

Now, while she pondered whether or not she should become the next International Minister of Education, she had plenty of time to catch up on the life everyone else thought she had missed out on.

She married the love of her life – a good man, college president of a historically Black College, who shared her passion for life-long learning and higher education, and together, they lived happily ever after, in the university's presidential mansion. And so did their quintuplets – who also possessed an acumen light years ahead of their peers!!!

Other Books By The Author!!!

Victoria Has A Secret

The Wealth Center

You Are A Jewel

The Luckiest Girl In Luckyville

What You Say To Your Child Really Does Matter

The Infinite Rules To Money

The Reading Specialist

Bibliography

Geer, P. Essential words for the gre (2013, 2010, 2007),
3rd Edition. Barron's Educational Series, Inc., New York.

Printed in the United States
By Bookmasters